Rail
by Rail

No. 1 The Hope Valley Line

Les Lumsdon
&
Martin Smith

Published by Platform 5 Publishing Limited, Lydgate House, Lydgate Lane, Sheffield S10 5FH

ISBN 0 906579 86 4

CONTENTS

◄A rare moment of peace and solitude on the main road through Castleton near to the Nags Head pub. On the right are just a few of the many tourist and jewellery shops to be found in the village. Above the shops looms Mam Tor.

Les Nixon

INTRODUCTION

Towering high above the mediaeval village of Castleton is the austere Peveril Castle, romanticised in Sir Walter Scott's 'Peveril of the Peak', but in reality being a harsh reminder of the Norman invasion nine hundred years ago. For many, this fortress marks the heartland of the Hope Valley and it was, for centuries, the protector of forested land used by the Norman overlords for hunting as well as for extracting minerals. The landscape is considerably different now, with distinctive drystone boundary walls breaking up sheep grazing pastures between isolated farmsteads. Not only do visitors come to admire this working countryside, for Castleton must surely have the largest concentration of show caves open to the public in Britain.

The Hope Valley can, with some justification, be called the 'Heart of the Peak District' and has always attracted attention. It was the expansion of Sheffield into the area, and the struggle about access to the high moors of Kinder Scout which led to the formation of the National Park in 1951 and the Hope Valley lies very much within its boundaries.

The Rivers

The valley stretches from the frowning face of Mam Tor in the west to the gritstone ramparts of Surprise View in the east. Its tributary valleys include the famous Edale, the less well known Bradwell Dale, Abney and Bretton Cloughs, and to the north the Upper Derwent and Alport valleys. In geographical terms, the main valley is actually that of the Derwent which enters the Hope Valley at Bamford and leaves it at Grindleford. The western arms of the valley are drained by Peakshole Water from Castleton and the River Noe from Edale, both offering beautiful stretches of water.

The Walks

For the walker the valley has something to suit most requirements, from the gentle riverside stroll to the rugged bog trotting hike on the high moors, or fine ridgeway rambles with unbelievable panoramic views. This book offers a selection of eighteen walks so that you can choose the rambles which best meet your inclination. Thus, there are a number of short walks for those who wish to while away an hour or two wandering along interesting and often beautiful paths. In this way, a family might enjoy an easily paced walk, stopping off at a village inn or cafe en route or to picnic nearby.

On the other hand, the book is ideal for those planning a longer day ramble or a weekend walk with an overnight stay at one of the numerous guesthouses, inns, campsites or Youth Hostel. By linking the walks outlined in the following chapters 1,4,7,10, and 14 you can walk the entire length of the Hope Valley. This will be particularly appealing to groups looking for a different angle for the Club or Society ramble.

The key idea of the book is to avoid circular walks to and from the car. All of the walks start and finish at a railway station. If travelling by car it is easy to catch the train to your chosen starting station and walk back to where you are parked. It also adds fun to the outing, especially for children who love train rides, even if they are literally hops from one station to the next. There's a seven day service on the Hope Valley line and with a little advance thinking the use of the train can enhance your walks. A number of circular walks have been included, however, and on the longer one way walks a few cut-off points have been suggested in case you become tired.

Maps and Clothing

Each walk includes a map and fairly explicit directions.

However, it makes sense to use maps wherever possible, preferably a 2½" to the mile scale (1:25000). The Hope Valley is covered by three sheets–The Dark Peak, The White Peak and the Pathfinder SK 28/38. While none of the walks involve extensive moorland walking it is essential that you are fully prepared for hill walking and are wary of changing weather conditions. It makes good sense to wear stout shoes or boots and to carry waterproofs in case the weather changes.

Always remember that even in the National Park you cannot simply wander at will everywhere. Stay on the footpaths, keep gates closed and respect the life of the countryside–take nothing but photographs, leave nothing but footprints. Most of all, enjoy your walking in the Hope Valley!

DORE TO GRINDLEFORD STATION

Dore, situated some 4 miles from central Sheffield, is the junction for the Hope Valley line. It is very much a dormitory area but is not without interest, for the Abbeydale Industrial Hamlet is less than ten minutes walk from the station. A visit to this restored 18th century hamlet makes for a really pleasant day out.

The walk begins in an urban area and climbs, steeply at time, to moorland. Towards Grindleford there are several woodland paths with a descent into the Derwent valley.

From Dore railway station turn left along the main road and continue for about three quarters of a mile until just before the railway bridge. At this point turn right along Totley Brook Road which parallels the railway line.

Where Totley Brook Road swings right near a police station, go left along a track, signed public footpath, over a bridge and alongside a stream. At Totley Grove the path skirts the grounds and comes into Hillfoot Road. Ignore the path crossing the bridge to your right. Hillfoot Road is narrow and has no verge so take care. Go left here, then right into Penny Lane by the Crown Inn. Penny Lane is also narrow but thankfully there is very little traffic.

Leaving The City Behind

At the Cricket Inn go left through a waymarked stile and make your way diagonally across the playing field so avoiding a bend in the road. Reaching the road again, go left, not forgetting to turn right up Moss Road and so leaving the city behind. You'll see the ventilator shafts of the Totley Tunnel here.

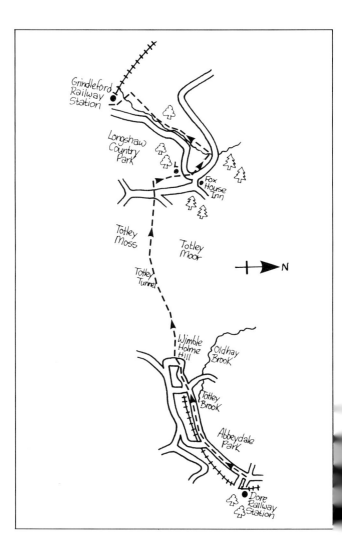

Totley Tunnel

At the first sharp bend in Moss Road, by the rifle range car park, go straight on through a waymarked stile up to another ventilator shaft. There are four shafts altogether for this tunnel. At 3½ miles in length, it is the longest land tunnel in the country. Three of the four shafts are at the eastern end as the landowner, the then Duke of Rutland, feared the smoke from them would affect his grouse on the open moorland. Not surprisingly, given the magnitude of the project, it took the engineers six years to build the Totley Tunnel.

The path rises steeply to rejoin the track which was formerly Moss Road and from here there is an excellent view back over Sheffield. Go left at the track which leads shortly through a gate and out onto open moor. The most noticeable feature of this part of the walk is the plethora of red Ministry of Defence signs warning of the nearby rifle range.

The path climbs steadily, easily but muddily onto the top of the moor and soon the fourth and deepest air shaft, about 800 feet, is sighted ahead, closely followed by a distant view of the summit of Sir William Hill and its television mast. These are good markers, but the track is clear anyway.

Longshaw Estate

Just before the air shaft is reached there is a fork in the path. Go left here and skirt to the south of the shaft. A further mile, often across wet sections, brings you to the junction of the B6055 and B6450 roads. Note ahead the wooden pole in the Longshaw Estate. This once served as a guide post in pack horse days and is useful as such even now. On the right you will see the prominent rock tors of Carl Wark. At the road go straight over and through a gate into the National Trust's Longshaw Estate and continue down to the well defined path running south to north. Go right along the foot of the boulary slope, until passing around the right side of Longshaw itself, the main driveway is reached and followed to the B6521 near Fox House Inn.

Padley Gorge

Go through the gate on the opposite side of the road and follow the path down through the wood, parallel to the main road and across the Burbage Brook, turn left and follow the well defined path beside the stream and into the oak woodland at the head of Padley Gorge. This area is a classic example of relict woodland, a survivor of a time whan all these hillsides were covered in dense deciduous forest. Changes in climate, the onset of man and changing grazing habits have reduced this extensive forest to tiny fragments, of which this is one. It too was threatened by sheep grazing during winter and spring, the young seedlings being eaten before they could grow large enough. Now sections of the wood are periodically fenced to allow new growth to flourish.

The path is good but ignore any deviations leftwards which go down and across the stream. Continue down the right hand side, past the Water Board building, until the edge of the wood is reached and there is a fine view down the Derwent Valley with the Eastern Edges on your left and Sir William Hill on the right. The track, now walled, goes steeply down to Upper Padley and a 'T' junction with a rough road. Turn left to Grindleford railway station. There is a cafe here which is open most days.

▶Padley Chapel is a prominent land mark close to Grindleford station. The building on the right is a National Park Ranger base whilst the scene is overlooked by Froggatt Edge.

Les Nixon

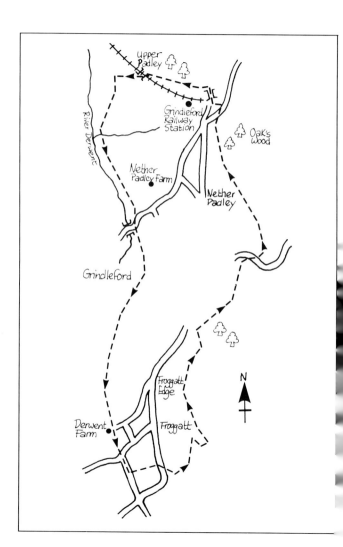

Upper
Padley

Grindleford
Railway
Station

Oak's
Wood

River Derwent

Nether
Padley Farm

Nether
Padley

Grindleford

Froggatt
Edge

Derwent
Farm

Froggatt

N

GRINDLEFORD TO FROGGATT CIRCULAR RAMBLE

Grindleford is a pleasantly situated station near to Padley Chapel and the Longshaw Estate. It also allows access to beautiful scenery and a number of gritstone edges, one of them being Froggatt Edge to the south.

The walk is easy, the only strenuous section being the climb up to Frogatt Edge. The views are excellent.

On leaving the railway station turn left and proceed down the rough lane passing by Padley Mill, noting the remains of the old waterwheel on the right. Continue along this lane which now comes parallel with the railway and you soon reach Padley Chapel.

Padley Chapel

The chapel commemorates the English Catholic Martyrs who were executed for their faith in the reign of the first Elizabeth. The chapel is now a place of pilgrimage.

A short distance ahead, the lane crosses a bridge, now heavily overgrown. This formerly carried our route over the tracks of the Derwent Valley Water Board's railway. This line was constructed in 1903 to bring stone down from Bole Hill quarries, some 300 feet higher up the hillside, to Grindleford where it was taken on the Hope Valley line to Bamford for the building of the Derwent Dams. The incline closed in 1910 and the line was dismantled.

Just over the bridge turn left and cross over the Hope Valley line by another bridge and enter a field. Follow the wall on your left until you find a stile just before a small copse. Go through this and cross the next field on a broad green path to its south west corner, where there is a gate.

13

Descend now, almost to the River Derwent, joining the riverside path where it crosses the Burbage Brook.

Horse Hay Coppice

Cross the brook and follow the well worn riverside path to the main B6521 road. Cross here and walk down towards the bridge. This was built in the days of turnpike roads and can now only accommodate single file traffic. Prior to the bridge go left through a kissing gate on to a footpath which is very often wet. This runs across the field slightly left to its southeast corner and soon enters Horse Hay Coppice. Coppicing is an old form of woodland management in which trees are not completely cleared but left as stumps to regenerate growth before re-cutting. In earlier times the timber produced was used in a wide variety of industries from charcoal making, for lead and iron smelting, to fencing. Coppicing, a human activity which encourages a rich wildlife, is little practised these days.

Follow this lovely path through the wood, keeping roughly in line with the river which you can see below. Eventually, the path emerges again into fields, four of which are crossed in succession until a narrow walled lane is entered. The lane has a centre line of paving slabs, evidence of this having been either a pack horse route or a better surface for a hard pressed cart horse. From the lane there is a fine view back up the valley towards Millstone Edge and Higger Tor, while looking south east the towering ramparts of Froggatt Edge now appear. You will see a prominent rock tower and a notch in the cliffs just to its right. Your way ahead lies through that notch!

Froggatt Village

You'll also see at this point, across the river, Stoke Hall quarry which produces dressed gritstone for building purposes, a contrast to the multi thousand tonne aggregate quarries to be found in the Buxton area. Further down the lane you'll see, on the other side of the river again, Stoke Hall itself with its equally impressive stable block. The lane becomes a tarmac road at Stonecroft and soon leads to Froggatt village. At the road junction by the Wesleyan Reform Chapel go straight ahead using the raised slabs or "causeys" provided and you soon come to another road junction hard by Froggatt Bridge. There's a well on the left before the bridge.

The bridge is a fine graceful structure with one pointed arch and a subsidiary rounded one. The pointed arch indicates to a mediaeval origin and the road width is barely sufficient for a car. It was almost certainly a crossing point for a packhorse route.

However, the walk does not cross the bridge, so at the junction proceed ahead until the road leaves the bank and begins to rise on route to Curbar. At a bend there is a gap between the houses on the left and a gate gives access to a field path which heads off steeply uphill. The way ahead is simple enough except that it can become very wet underfoot as you walk up to the main B6054 road just to the right of The Chequers Inn.

Cross the road and go over the stile into the Bee Wood, but why it has such a name is not immediately apparent. The path climbs up steeply changing steadily from a south easterly to north easterly direction. A breather can be taken at the stile in the wall, beyond which the trees begin to thin out and the views over the Derwent valley are considerable.

Froggatt Edge

Finally clearing the trees, the path reaches a pronounced terrace at the foot of the cliffs of Froggatt Edge. The rock tower, seen earlier from a distance, is now on your left and even more impressive. The notch, through which your path

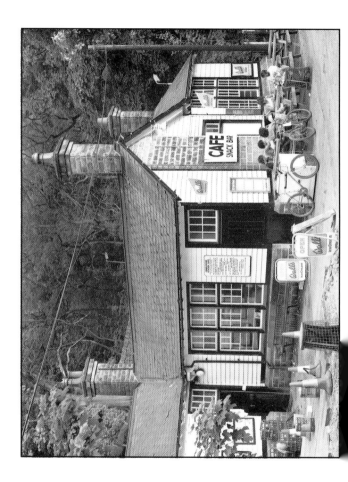

passes, is on the right. The view along the Derwent valley is most impressive, from Hathersage in the north to beyond Chatsworth House to the south. Your way is to the right, up through the notch to join the broad highway along the top of the edge. Turn left and lake your way to the first outcrop, which is adjacent to the top of the rock tower.

The route along the edge is an easy stroll with superb views. Keep your eyes peeled for a stone circle lying close to the path on your right. It is easily missed. Eventually, the path reaches the main B6054 road. Cross this with care as the visibility is limited and go through a kissing gate on your left. the path descends a flight of steps to the brook. Cross it and go through the gap in the wall to a stile. Cross this and keep to the left hand path. Go over another stile by the electricity transmission pylon and follow the wide path past disused quarries. There are occasional glimpses to your left of Grindleford Bridge far below and a distant view up the Derwent to Win Hill and Kinder Scout beyond. Continue to walk along the wider path avoiding paths veering off steeply downhill. Your route now begins to descend gently and soon reaches a gate and stile adjacent to a National Trust notice.

Follow the track onwards and downwards until a road is reached. Go right here along the road ignoring the footpath indicating Froggatt Edge road. Your route soon reaches the main road B6521 road. Cross the main road and turn right here, then go over the stream by a bridge and then left down a roughly surfaced path. This leads unerringly down to Grindleford station.

◀For most walkers and ramblers a cup of tea is most welcome and one pleasant stop is the old station buildings at Grindleford now used as a cafe. Surprisingly the structure has been little altered since it was sold by British Rail almost twenty years ago.   *Les Nixon*

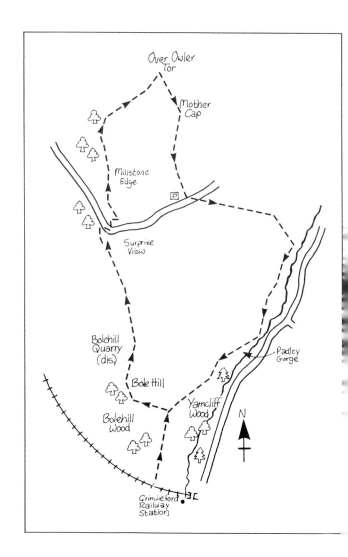

Over Owler Tor

Mother Cap

Millstone Edge

Surprize View

Bolehill Quarry (dis.)

Bole Hill

Padley Gorge

Yarncliff Wood

Bolehill Wood

N

Grindleford Railway Station

WALK THREE: Approximately 3 miles (5 km)

GRINDLEFORD TO OWLER TOR AND PADLEY GORGE CIRCULAR RAMBLE

A splendid walk through ancient woodland and along impressive rocky edges. A steep climb at first over indistinct paths but there are no serious difficulties. The walk will be of interest to those who enjoy industrial archaelogy.

On leaving the station go left and proceed down the rough lane passing by Padley Mill. Beyond the mill the track climbs and swings to the right. At the top of the rise another track turns off to the right to a number of houses. Although not shown on your map this is a recognised path into the National Trust property surrounding Padley Gorge. Go up this track, which climbs very steeply, and pass a curious crescent shaped pond on the left, eventually reaching a gate and a stile leading into National Trust land.

Go through the stile and make your way up to the Derwent Valley Water Board building. Its unusual design with a rounded roof instantly mark it out as part of the vast Derwent Dams construction project in the early part of this century. The building marks the line of the aquaduct which skirts around the north side of Grindleford before passing below the edges, through Chatsworth Park to Amblegate, Nottingham and Leicester.

Bole Hill Wood

Keep to the left of the building and follow the narrow path up, through a stile and into Bole Hill Wood, a mixture of oak, birch and beech. Shortly, the path climbs up onto a terrace, but simply crosses it and climbs once again up the bank on the other side. This terrace is also a remnant of

the reservoir building era at the turn of the century. It was once a part of the railway line serving Bole Hill quarries. Stone was conveyed down an inclined plane to the Hope Valley railway line at Grindleford and then to Bamford and the main construction site at Birchinlee.

Continue upwards along this path, which is narrow but distinct on the ground. It weaves its way up through a maze of abandoned quarry workings, now completely overgrown by trees until it levels and peters out. A narrow cutting rises up to the left. Follow this to emerge above the trees with a fine view up the Hope Valley to Win Hill and beyond. At the top of the cutting the path recommences and goes off right towards the prominent rocks seen on the skyline.

Old Quarry Workings

The path enters another area of birch thicket, weaving about through overgrown quarry workings, but fortunately it is now a wide and distinct route. These are far older workings and there are examples of dressed stone remaining, in particular a large stone trough which can be seen amongst the trees. Watch out for ant hills on this section; it is not the spot for a nap!

Millstones Everywhere

Eventually a path joins from the right just below a jumble of rocks and your way ahead is through two stone gate posts slightly to the left. Immediately on passing these posts you are confronted with a pile of millstones and examples of other dressed stonework. There must be well over a hundred of them, making a most unusual sight.

Continue along the trackway which is well engineered and easily graded, up towards the main road. Again, the view

◀ Close to the site of the abandoned Bole Hill Quarry and the Surprise View high above Hathersage can be found dozens of partly fashioned millstones. If any one could find a modern day use for these they would undoubtedly make a small fortune!   Les Nixon

21

of the Hope Valley opens up to your left taking in Abney Clough, the television mast on Sir William Hill and the chimney of Ladywash Mine close to it. Ladywash mine shaft was 700 feet deep, almost the deepest lead mine in Derbyshire. Latterly, fluorspar was mined there but became uneconomic. The buildings and headgear were demolished in 1984.

Reaching the main road, go right, ignoring the two obvious tracks opposite. Go past the bend and wandering sheep signs. Just before the bend itself cross the road with care and follow a terrace to the left, below the rocks for about 50 metres. A narrow path then slants up to the right to a stile. Go up this path and over the stile. Then turn left and follow the post and wire fence as it skirts the edges of the rocks. The higher you climb the better the view along the valley and also over the moorlands to Sheffield.

Millstone Edge

This edge is known as Millstone Edge, indicative of the great industry that took place here in earlier decades and in previous centuries. The quarries themselves were preceded by what was known as daystone working and there are remains of this ancient stone working method scattered all over this area of moorland.

Continue onwards and upwards until finally the summit is reached. The northern panorama opens up with Higger Tor prominent, away to the north east beyond a series of little tors known as Winyards Nick. The jumbled pile of rock closest to you is Over Owler Tor and it is to this point that the walk now proceeds. Keep alongside the fence for a short while then when it starts to dip away make for the tor, following the erratic but obvious sheep tracks. The easiest way is to climb the rocks just to the south of the tor itself, then make your way up to the summit for some magnificent views and entertaining scrambles.

Mother Cap

Head south now for Mother Cap, a huge monolith of curiously shaped stone. The path is obvious underfoot though there are numerous half hidden boulders so take care. Beyond Mother Cap the path becomes indistinct but head for the car park which now comes into view.

Pass through a new thicket of birch scrub and a stile appears to the left of the car park. Go over this stile to emerge onto the main A625 road. Cross the road with care and descend into the hollow through the two stone gate posts. Here, you will find a kissing gate, not visible from the road above, and the start of a deeply cut packhorse way. Follow this until you reach a large boulder where another path crosses. Go right along this path out of the hollow way and onto the moor. A broad green swathe leads towards the stream but becomes far less distinct as you near the brook. Ignore the clearer cross paths. Almost at the stream, follow the riverside path, right, downstream to Padley Gorge.

Padley Gorge

The woodland in the gorge is ancient, being a relic of times when much of the Peak District was forested. Recent overgrazing by sheep has, however, severely limited the natural regeneration of the wood. Further on, you'll notice a fenced area to your right with a plentiful growth of young trees. This is an experimental plot, part of a research project organised by Sheffield University designed to test the effects of excluding grazing in such woodland. It seems very effective!

The path through the wood is delightful, near to the fast flowing river cascading down the gorge. Ignore all paths to your left and continue ahead, climbing slightly to pass a ruinedstone building on the right. Descend to the round roofed Water Board building you passed on the outward journey. Retrace your steps back to Grindleford railway station.

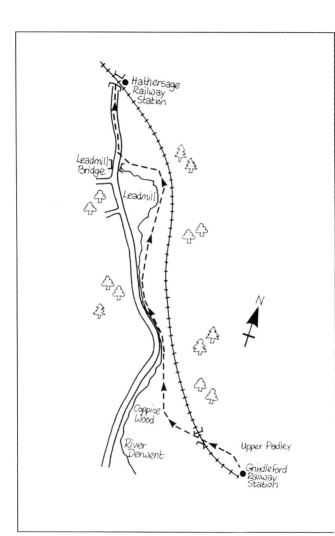

WALK FOUR: Approximately 2 miles (3 km)

GRINDLEFORD TO HATHERSAGE STATION

This is an easy riverside walk with no gradients to speak of and although the path is well worn in places and muddy in wet weather, the beautiful Derwent is compensation enough.

As in Walk Two, turn left and follow the rough track beyond Padley Chapel, over the old Water Board railway trackbed and left over the Hope Valley railway line. Follow the wall to your left until it turns right near a small copse. After crossing three fields towards the railway it enters Coppice Wood, still remaining on the left hand side of the tracks. The path decends to meet another distinct riverside path in the wood.

The River Derwent

The Derwent is Derbyshire's principal river, rising as it does in the far north of the country and then bisecting it as it journeys south to the Trent near Shardlow. Its name derives from the Celtic, meaning river by the oak woods – a beautiful name for a beautiful river and it is at its best on this walk.

The path is well used and follows the river bank, beyond the wood, for two fields before veering away from the Derwent for a short distance. It then rejoins the river bank for the final section, emerging to the right of Leadmill Bridge near to Hathersage. The name of the bridge is indicative of the type of industry carried out on here in times past. Water power was harnessed for the bellows at this lead smelter. This represented a great technological leap from the primitive 'boles', early smelters found on the windswept eastern edges. Hence the name Bole Hill as mentioned in Walk Three.

From Leadmill Bridge your way to Hathersage is to the right along the main B6001 road to the railway station. There is a footpath alongside the road and once under the bridge the station entrance is on the right. For Hathersage continue ahead. To the left at Leadmill Bridge is a short walk up to the Plough Inn. Over the bridge there is a stile leading onto another clearly defined riverside path leading to Bamford so the walk can easily be extended using this way if required.

WALK FIVE: Approximately 7 miles (11 km)

HATHERSAGE TO BRETTON CIRCULAR RAMBLE

Hathersage is a fine Peakland village with a range of shops, catering establishments and a swimming pool. Its chief claims to fame, in terms of tourism attraction, are its association with Charlotte Bronte and its even older association with the legends of Robin Hood, Little John being buried in the churchyard.

The walk is an interesting excursion into one of the lesser used valleys in the Peak Park. There is some climbing and the walk is not distinct on the ground in a few places but this should not deter the adventurous. The scenery is very exciting.

Leave the station along the approach road and at the junction with the main B6001 road turn left. Cross the road and go under the bridge with care as there is no footway until the other side. Continue down the road to Leadmill Bridge. There was a lead smelter here in the early eighteenth century and widened in 1928, but this was a much earlier crossing point over the Derwent, known as Hazelford.

Continue along the main road to the junction opposite The Plough Inn. Go right here along a much quieter lane with some fine views of the surrounding valley. After a short distance the lane bears right and a track continues ahead by a milk churn loading platform. Follow the track, which contours around the shoulder of the hill to enter the valley of Highlow Brook. Soon, a footpath sign is reached and resisting the temptation to continue on the near level track through Broadhey Farm, instead follow the sign to the left, diagonally down the hillside through the thorn thicket, to emerge by the Highlow Brook.

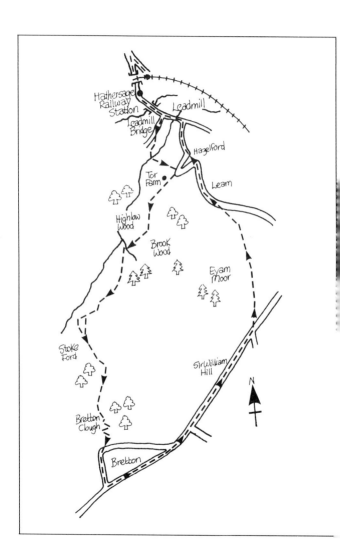

Highlow Brook

The path is obvious enough but is very damp in places and leads to a bridge over the Highlow Brook. Over the bridge another footpath sign directs you to Stoke Ford, by a path leading off left up a slanting terrace in the hillside. Where the terrace reaches the field boundary simply follow the wall up past Hog Hall, which is actually a very nice house, to a gate and stile which leads into a rough, walled lane. Continue up this lane until it joins another lane at a complicated T junction. Go right here, following another rough lane towards Tor Farm. Here, the track swings to the right into the farmyard but you go straight on, through a gate into fields again.

There follows a very pleasant stretch of trackway, with close cropped turf underfoot. The route continues alongside the wall through the first field then marches straight through the middle of the second and third fields with lovely views over the Highlow valley to Highlow Hill opposite. The name seems contradictory! However, 'low' is a common place name in Derbyshire, meaning hill and deriving from the Norse word 'hlaw'. Pass a spring, with stone trough and continue to the gate at the entrance to Highlow Wood. This wood is mainly larch and as the path descends towards the stream it becomes more of a muddy scramble.

At the stream the path crosses a stile. On the right is a simple plank bridge alongside a ford. Do not go over the bridge but instead the tributary stream using the boulder provided and ascend the worn farm tractor-way up the spur between the two brooks. The tractor ruts belie the age of this route, which is one of numerous packhorse tracks in the area. Follow the track as it climbs steadily away from Highlow Brook onto open hillside. The view down the valley is good, Millstone Edge being particularly prominent.

Stoke Ford

Do not follow the tractor route climbing the flanks of Bole Hill, but near two lonely thorn trees leave this tractor-way and follow a broad green path down to the right towards the river again. As the path descends to Stoke Ford it enters an area of scrub woodland. The ford and the attendant footbridge can be seen below. Go down to the ford but do not cross. Bear left and then keep right into Bretton Clough. It is most important to bear right at this point than going off up the prominent zig zag path.

As you walk up Bretton Clough you will find the path narrow but well defined. There is one difficult spot where a spring has to be avoided. The path shortly goes over a stile and swings into a deep tributary clough. Without losing much height at all the stream is crossed and a broad green path rises steeply on the opposite side, passing a ruined farmstead. The walked path here keeps to open fields rather than the route noted on the Ordnance Survey map, until it enters the area of scrub and meets a very wet section. Most walkers skirt it and the path is picked up again turning into another deep tributary clough.

The right of way joins by a slanting terrace on the left and the two routes combine and descend to a stile. Cross the stile and negotiate a stream and another wet patch. The path makes a bee line for the foot of a curiously shaped conical hill then zig zags left. This section of route is a

◀The Barrel Inn on Bretton Edge must enjoy one of the finest locations in the Peak District if not the country. The inn is a pleasant place to stop to enjoy scenery and refreshments.

Les Nixon

classic packhorse way and climbs to Bretton up the steep hillside. Follow the path up the tributary clough, in a worn hollow, then zig-zagging right and eventually ascending through a short cutting to emerge into an open area. There are superb views from here. Follow the route left to a stile then go by the path, with the wall to the right, towards the house ahead. Cross another stile by a gate.

Bretton

This leads onto a rough lane which soon joins a tarmac road. This quiet lane passes Bretton Youth Hostel and emerges by the Barrel Inn, which welcomes walkers but can be very busy at weekends . The inn is perched on Bretton Edge, which here is surprisingly narrow and steep sided. To the south the land falls away to the limestone plateau of the central Peak District, to the north it drops to Bretton Clough. To the west it tapers to Hucklow Edge, a haunt for gliding enthusiasts and eastwards the land rises to the mast crowned summit of Sir William Hill.

As the notice board outside the pub relates, this is an ancient highway. At the time of the turnpiking of roads in the eighteenth century this was chosen as the main route between Sheffield and Buxton until superceded first by the Eyam road and then by the current main road through Middleton Dale.

Sir William Hill

Leaving the Barrel go left, along this road in the direction of Sir William Hill. "Who is Sir William?", you are no doubt asking yourself by now. The answer is open to dispute. The place name is first recorded in 1692, at which time there was a Sir William Cavendish owning nearby Stoke Hall but there was also Sir William Saville not too far away at the Manor of Eyam. One thing seems certain though, is that it was unlikely to have been named after Sir William Bagshawe in spite of the pub sign in Grindleford

As you draw near the top of the hill so the vista becomes quite spectacular. Where the tarmac road turns right go straight ahead along the broad and stony lane. This was turnpike road mentioned earlier, which was abandoned in 1795. The summit of this lane is in a shallow cutting and the view ahead opens up with a great sweep of the gritstone edges. To the right can be seen the chimney of the former Ladywash Mine, formerly worked for lead then fluorspar.

Descending, you come to the junction with the tarmac Eyam road. Two paths go off left here. Take the second and go over the stile onto the moor. The path is easily followed, alongside a fence which divides the moorland from 'improved' pasture. Eventually this path leaves the fence and striking across the open moor heads straight for the prominent bulk of Higger Tor.

Drunken Gateposts

On reaching two drunken gateposts in a derelict wall, the path now turns north and begins to descend rapidly towards Hathersage. Eventually it reaches the Leam road at a gate and stile. Go over the stile and bear left down the road. Continue along this quiet lane until it takes a sharp turn to the left. Proceed ahead here through a stile by the telegraph pole, to descend steeply in a narrow hollow way out into a field. The path continues over another stile to the left of the fine old house, Hazelford Hall, and rejoins the road.

Go right at the tarmac lane and just past the farm buildings go up the rickety step stile on the right and follow the footpath parallel to the main road. This was commonplace in the days when the lanes were so deep in mud as to be impassable to mere walkers. Why not keep up good traditions, especially in this case as the road is fairly narrow with no verges! At the main road go left to the Plough Inn and retrace your steps to Hathersage.

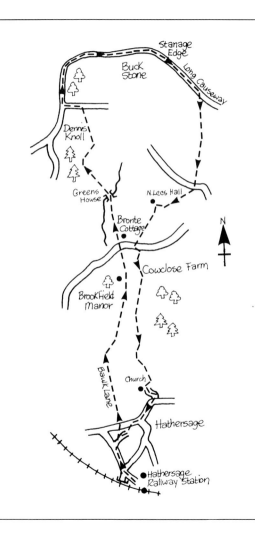

HATHERSAGE TO STANAGE EDGE

This walk takes you through Hathersage, with an opportunity to look in the church to see the fine Eyre brasses or to visit little John's grave. The climax of the walk is the impressive Stanage Edge. There are several climbs but the path is clear to follow in most places.

Go down the station approach and at the main road turn right towards the village centre. Pass the austere looking Moorlands House on the right, then at the next junction turn right along Oddfellows Road, where there is an open air swimming pool and cafe. Cross the road and where it bends right, proceed along a path ahead, by a green lamp post, between some unusual buildings to the main A625 road. Cross with care and go down the lane directly opposite which is signed 'To the church'.

Stroll along this lane passing by the cricket pitch and scout hut until it reaches the house called Lane End where the track becomes a field access way. This track crosses a series of fields and Stanage is always in view ahead, while behind is the spire of Hathersage church and beyond, Highlow Hill.

Brookfield Manor

Soon Brookfield Manor comes into view to your left. It is now a business training centre. The track heads for Cowclose Farm but your way slants to the left in the direction of the Manor as indicated by the finger post. Follow this path, which shortly crosses a stile and becomes a well built modern version of a causeway running at the back of the new manorial buildings. North Lees Hall can just be discerned on the hillside to the right, half hidden by trees. The new footway is enclosed by fences until it joins the

35

tradesmens' drive to the manor. Keep right, following the signs, past the disused house and over the stream onto a track leading to a gate which gives out onto Birley Lane.

Cross Birley Lane and go over the stile into the fields. Keep left on the broad green path parallel to the stream leading to a narrow gate entering the wood. Looking right, the arched remains of a chapel can be seen just to the left of North Lees Hall. The chapel enjoyed a brief but turbulent existence in the time of James II before being sacked by Protestant locals who objected to its Catholic presence.

Follow the path through the wood until a footbridge is reached by the confluence of two streams. Go over the bridge and climb the path on the opposite bank alongside the little tributary brook. The rising path soon leads out of the wood at a kissing gate and enters open fields. The path, not too obvious underfoot, rises across the field to another kissing gate to the right of the main field gate. Go through the kissing gate and follow the fence to a stile near Greens House. Go left here, through the gateway and at the house follow the signed footpath right, through another gate, into a walled green lane. The walling on the left soon gives way to drop to a stream. Go over another stile and the lane disgorges onto an open moor.

The Long Causeway

At this point go right, following the boundary wall until a gateway is reached and a track comes in from the left. Go through the gateway and continue alongside the wall again.

A view of the village of Hathersage and in the distance Stanage Edge seen through the tracery of leafless branches close to the River Derwent. Features of particular interest are the church, top right, and Nether Hall at the left of the picture.

Les Nixon

Stanage Edge is now very prominent to the right. At a blocked up gateway cross the stile. The Long Causeway, thought to be Roman in origin, can be seen slanting up to cross the Edge. Continue to follow the wall as it meets the fir trees of the plantation at Dennis Knoll and it soon reaches the road at a cattle grid. Go left over the grid, ignoring the narrow trod leading away right, and continue on the road for a short distance until it turns sharp left. Your way is to the right along a track, The Long Causeway which leads up to Stanage Edge. There's a fine view of Hathersage and other surrounding edges.

The Buck Stone

As the ascent continues, the track draws alongside a curious walled depression on the right, containing a number of large boulders, of which the largest is the Buck Stone. It was once probably an overnight shelter for 'jaggers', the men who led the packhorse trains through these hills. Notice the notches in the Buck Stone. These, apparently were for the 'jaggers' to rest poles, thus forming a crude shelter. The boggy area was presumably a watering area for the ponies.

Continue up the main track onto the highest piece of embankment and onto the Edge itself. The views are quite exhilarating, including a full panorama of the Hope Valley. At the 'Boundary of Open Country' sign leave the causeway to pursue its way to Sheffield and go right over the stile and along the Edge itself. This is easy but exciting walking. At the first rock formation on the left, with a grotesquely carved rock closest to the edge path, look right and a paved way can be seen zig-zagging its way down the cliffs and into a plantation. Locate the top of the path by the rock mentioned and follow its easy gradients down to the wood.

The entrance to the wood is by way of an odd shaped gateway. The paving continues through the wood, being a fine example of a restored packhorse 'causey'. Emerging from the woodland, the path descends towards the car park. At the two big boulders the path splits into three. Go left towards the mountain rescue post. On reaching the road, go straight ahead through the gateway to the left of the mountain rescue post into a plantation and pick up a roughly paved path which leads down to a clear track descending to North Lees. On reaching this track go right and follow the way down to a stile while the stream to your left cascades over a series of miniature waterfalls. Once over the stile and out of the woodland keep on the broad green path as it heads towards North Lees Hall.

Charlotte Brontë

This fine old hall, now in the hands of the Peak National Park, was once in the hands of the Eyre family. The legend is that Robert Eyres, who lived at Highlow Hall, built houses for each of his seven sons, North Lees being one of them. North Lees is also associated with the Brontës and in particular, Charlotte Brontë. In the famous novel Jane Eyre, Hathersage became Morton and North Lees, the residence of the tortured Mr Rochester. Charlotte stayed at Hathersage with a friend whose brother was the local vicar, again represented in the story. It all seems quite plausible.

Go forward through a gate and descend the steps on your left to skirt around the left side of the hall in a walled lane until you reach a tarmac drive. Follow this to the road and go left then right by the sheep sign and through a gate onto a track. This leads to Cowclose farm. At the farm skirt the buildings to the left through a small gate and so regain the track, a diversion not shown on the map but obviously used by many ramblers as the dogs bark louder! Beyond the farm the track soon disappears and the way becomes a green path running alongside a hedge and fence. At the end of the wood, after crossing a spring, go over stile. A well defined terrace continues straight ahead, but the path now slants right to a stile where Hathersage church comes into view.

Head directly towards the church descending now to cross a small stream. Climb steeply up the far bank and onto a green lane. Go left and this emerges on the tarmac road by the church. Follow this to the main road, passing by The Scotsman's Pack public house, where you turn right. Proceed along the main road for short distance then by the little grocery shop, cross the road and go up the access to the right of the shop, skirting to the right past the rear of the next building to pick up a signed footpath. This runs in front of some beautifully kept gardens to emerge in Oddfellows Road. Go right here and retrace your steps to the station.

HATHERSAGE TO BAMFORD STATION

A walk mainly across fields with gentle climbs only. The path crosses a golf course so some care is needed when golfers are at full swing. The walk offers pleasant valley landscapes.

As in Walk Six bear right from the station entrance and then after Moorlands House into Oddfellows Road. As the road bends to the right go ahead through an old pathway behind a set of interesting buildings. This leads to the main A625 road and you cross by The Hathersage Inn. The village shops and cafes are to the left here. Walk directly up the path signed 'To The Church' and pass by the cricket ground. If you are visiting the church use the path on the right signed 'Wet Weather Route to the Church'. The diversion is only a matter of minutes.

Hathersage Church

The church contains a number of brasses of the local Eyre family mentioned in Walk Six, but it is also famous for its associations with the Robin Hood stories. Legend has it that Little John is buried in the graveyard and until the nineteenth century Little John's bow and Lincoln green cap were hung in the church but have long since vanished. There is, however, a memorial in the churchyard to the gentle giant. Retrace your steps to the track by the cricket ground and turn right.

Not far beyond the scout hut go left through a stile and cut across a field to the right where you'll find a footbridge over Hood Brook. Once clear of the stream walk directly up the bank following the line of trees to a lonely stile. Cross this and after a few metres bear right across the field to another stile, not noticeable at first, which leads to a

41

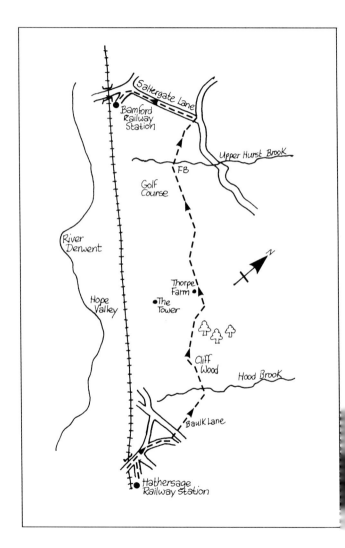

tarmac road. Turn right and then, after a short distance, left at the lane which is signposted to Bamford.

Beware of the Balls

You soon pass by Thorpe Farm over a stone stile to the right and then skirting round take a direction slightly to the left and downhill to a stile. The path now leads down to a brook. Cross over and continue upwards to a golf course. The right of way continues ahead but it makes sense to keep near to the hedge in order to avoid those little white missiles. The course is broken up by the Upper Hurst Brook. At the green before the brook bear right down to the footbridge. The path curves gently upwards again and maintains a course near to the hedge. At a point near the number 2 green you bear gently right to a stile in the corner of the course which leads to a tarmac lane.

Turn left and follow this lane the short distance to Bamford railway station which is on the left once at the main A6013 road.

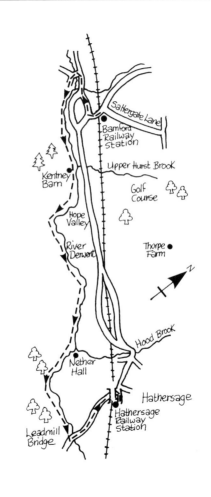

WALK EIGHT: Approximately 2 miles (3 km)

BAMFORD TO HATHERSAGE STATION

An easy riverside walk mainly along the side of the Derwent. Care has to be taken in places where the river has eroded the steep sided banks. This can be combined with Walk 7 to make a circular ramble from Hathersage.

From Bamford railway station turn left towards The Marquis of Granby public house, named after Sir John Manners, a venerated soldier in The Seven Years War. At the first junction go right by the gateposts and walk along the old access road to the main A625 to Castleton. These gateposts were from a turnpike toll gate which controlled the Hope and Bamford road in earlier times. They have been restored here for passers by to view when on their travels but no toll is now collected.

Turn right and walk over the footbridge by the Mytham Bridge and by the garden centre. Cross the road and turn first left into a lane signposted 'To Shatton'. Within yards turn left again through a stile, across a footbridge and climbing up the wooded riverbanks where the River Noe meets the Derwent.

Riverside Walk

Your way is ahead now along the Derwent, using a well worn path which can become very wet in Winter. There are numerous stiles but they are not mentioned in the text as the path is very straightforward, simply keeping company with the delightful Derwent for the entire length. After another footbridge the path drops to a flat riverside meadows with Kentney Barn ahead and Glover Bank climbing away to your right. The river sweeps to the right after this landmark and once again you cross a clough, and climb

45

through woodland, before reaching the floodplain.

Woodland Sections

You pass several field boundaries and in places are fenced in close to the riverside. Pass by Nether Hall on the opposite bank and eventually cross Dunge Brook and enjoy another beautiful woodland section. Finally, you reach a level grassy path leading to Leadmill Bridge, where you turn left for Hathersage railway station or right for the Plough Inn at Leadmill.

◄The broad sweep of the charming valley between Hathersage and Bamford. The latter village is just off the picture to the left while the footpath follows the far side of the large field seen in the middle distance. *Les Nixon*

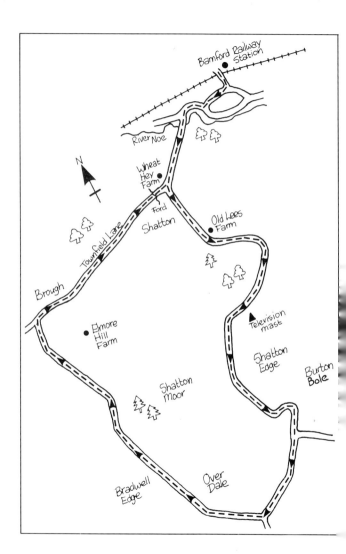

WALK NINE: Approximately 6/7 miles (11 km)

BAMFORD TO SHATTON EDGE CIRCULAR RAMBLE

Bamford, the name deriving from Beamford, is a pleasant settlement with a few shops, inns and a garden centre. It holds a very popular Sheep Dog Trials every year drawing contestants from the valley and beyond.

The walk is fairly easy going with one or two steep climbs.

On leaving Bamford station by the steps from the platform, turn left as in Walk Eight and follow the old road to the main A625 road and cross to the lane signposted to Shatton. Make your way up through Shatton until the junction with Townfield Lane is reached where you go left by a ford and continue up past Nether Shatton Farm and so leave the hamlet behind.

The lane now begins to ascend very steeply towards the television mast visible high above. The route of the walk is very clear. It follows Shatton Lane all of the way around Overdale, but the way is steep. Stop for a breather to admire the views over Win Hill and Ladybower.

Early Smelting

The lane makes a pronounced east-west zig zag and then reaches the television mast. Here the surface becomes much rougher underfoot and the lane, still climbing, rounds the end of Shatton Edge and turns left. The valley on the right is Overdale, part of which is a nature reserve. The hillside to the left is Burton Bole, a bole being a place where lead was smelted before the advent of more sophisticated 'Cupola' furnaces.

The gradient now eases and the track swings left for a short way to reach the junction of rough lanes. Go right here

49

and follow the track which is now virtually level and with excellent views.

Continue along the track, ignoring the tarmac road leading off left to Abney. Shortly, the track swings to the right and various paths join here. Ignore all of these and continue along the walled lane which now begins to descend towards Brough, opening up a magnificent panorama of the Hope Valley.

Navio

Descending steeply, the lane passes the access to Elmore Hill Farm. The village of Brough can be seen below and in the fields beyond, a raised square area of ground, partly delineated by a fence and trees, marks the site of Navio, the Roman fortress. The Roman road from Brough to Glossop can be seen clearly across the valley, slanting up the flanks of Win Hill towards Hope Cross.

You soon come to a T junction where you turn right and follow the walled lane until it becomes a track across fields. This is reputedly another Roman road, this time destined for Templeborough (Rotherham).

The way is obvious throughout and the field track, after climbing again for a short distance, levels out and soon becomes a walled lane which dips steadily to enter Shatton village at the junction by the ford. There is a raised causeway and footbridge for those not wanting wet feet. Here, the outward route is rejoined for the short walk to Bamford station.

BAMFORD TO EDALE STATION

This fine walking route takes you alongside Ladybower Reservoir through magnificent scenery, then over ancient packhorse trails into the Vale of Edale. The walking is easy but allow the best part of a day.

Leave the railway station entrance and turn right along the main A6013 road into Bamford village. Just beyond the garage, ignore a footpath sign to the left, but continue until a lane leads off left, signed Severn Trent Water Authority. Descend to cross the River Derwent by way of a girder bridge. Follow this tarmac lane for a short while until it reaches an imposing building on the right. This was formerly the headquarters of the Derwent Valley Water Board.

Beyond the offices, a path leads off to the right to a cutting alongside the offices. This is the trackbed of the Birchinglee and Tintown railway, built to convey materials and men for the construction of the Derwent and Howden Dams. In use from 1902 to 1914 it was dismantled only to be partly rebuilt again for construction of the Ladybower dam from 1935 to 1945.

The path soon leaves the trackbed climbing away to the left. Follow this clearly defined path up to Thornhill village where you turn right on the tarmac road and right at the next junction. This road leads up to Ladybower reservoir. Some ramblers, however, stay on the trackbed and this leads to the road and then to the dam itself. Either way you come to a track at the western end of Ladybower Dam.

Dam Building

The old railway embankment continues across the track to disappear into the dam itself. It is hard to imagine that the

51

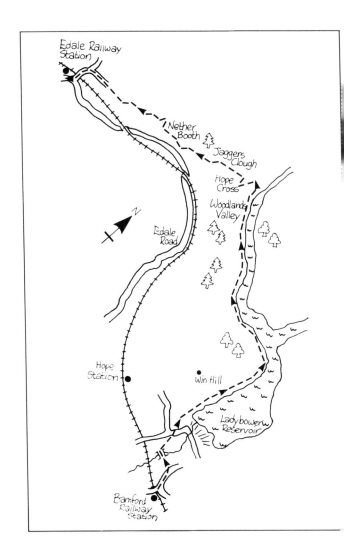

valley below was once a sight of feverish constructional activity fifty years ago, with narrow gauge engines scurrying backwards and forwards with trainloads of spoil and materials.

Leave the railway line and walk up the track to the left to the crest of the dam and your first view of the vast expanse of Ladybower. A glorious 3 miles now follows on a well defined track following the side of the reservoir for most part. The track gradually swings to the left to enter the Woodlands Valley with stunning views over the water to Ashopton Viaduct. It then briefly climbs away from the waterside through the plantations but keep to the right hand paths at all times and soon you descend to the waters edge again. You'll see a low tunnel entrance on your left as you progress. This brings water from the River Noe in Edale through to Ladybower reservoir.

At a point where an old road emerges from the lake and joins the track, go left on a pathway which slants up into the trees. The path climbs easily but somewhat damply to the remains of a farm which is now utterly derelict. The path makes a sharp left turn here rising above the ruins. As the trees gradually thin, the views open up again over Derwent Edge and Crooks Hill. Still rising, the path emerges from the wood over a gate to reach Hope Cross.

Hope Cross

The inscriptions on the four faces read Glossop, Edale, Hope, and Derwent. The present guide stone is a replacement of the mediaeval cross which served this important function of early trackways. Go up the Roman road in the direction of Glossop for a short distance then, at the wall and gate (the true 'crossroads'), go left along the clearly defined path which soon begins to descend steeply into Jagger's Clough.

Jagger's Clough

Jagger is the name for a packhorse man and it is easy to see why this clough got its name as there are numerous hollow ways leading down to a stream crossing and then up the other side.

Edale Youth Hostel

On reaching the crest of the spur out of Jagger's Clough the track begins to dip into Edale. Care is now needed, for the main path carries on down through Clough Farm and onto the road. The route you need skirts around to the right side of the farm on a narrow path, which is not

The view of Edale from a point close to the popular Youth Hostel in the valley. In this scene looking south west the hill on the left is Mam Tor, perhaps one of its least imposing aspects. *Les Nixon*

readily identified. Sometimes a sign to the Youth Hostel is present, sometimes it is not! Follow the path around Clough Farm and round the flank of the hill into Lady Booth Clough. The building on the opposite side of the clough is Edale Youth Hostel and the path dips down to cross the brook and into the hostel grounds.

The Edale path is waymarked through the grounds. Don't follow the main drive but skirt around the front of the building to a stile and follow an almost level route across a series of fields, around the back of Woodhouse Farm where the path begins to descend into an irregularly shaped field. As this field is entered the path becomes indistinct so head for the right hand boundary and follow this down to a stile in the bottom right hand corner of the field. Here the path from Nether Booth to Ollerbrook Booth is joined. Go right here towards Ollerbrook Booth and after several fields and stiles the access track to Cotefield is joined and followed to Ollerbrook Booth.

The place name 'Booth' is common in these parts denoting the site of a former temporary residence for shepherds and the like. Continue ahead through Ollerbrook Booth, ignoring the lane to the left. Just by the last building the path splits. Take the left hand path, which is very clearly defined, to the Peak Park Information Centre and to Edale railway station by the very welcome Rambler Inn or the cafe on the other side of the bridge.

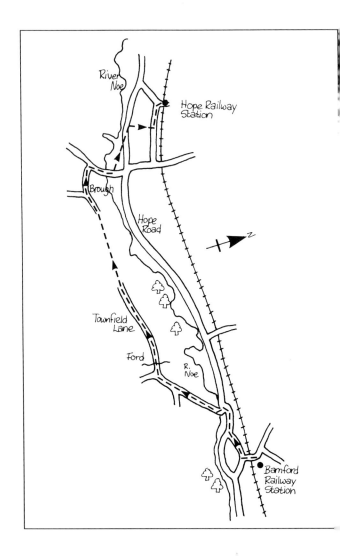

WALK ELEVEN: Approximately 3 miles (5 km)

BAMFORD TO HOPE STATION

This short walk along easy tracks is by no means exacting but offers views across the gentler slopes of the Hope Valley.

As in Walk Nine make your way to Shatton Lane. Follow this through Shatton, ignoring the first lane on the left. Then, where the lane forks, go right over the ford and climb away from the valley bottom though still parallel to the river. The views across the valley are magnificent. This was the former Roman road from Navio to Templeborough. Eventually, the lane became no more than a track, passes Upper Shatton and the mouth of Over Dale, one of the least known Derbyshire dales, before becoming a tarmac lane once again at the T junction.

Brough

Follow this road steeply down to Brough. On your left you will see the village well, sometimes named as St Annes Well. In the village go right along the main B6049 road, once a Roman way known as Batham Gate, towards the main A625 near to the Traveller's Rest public house.

Just over the bridge beyond the mill, go left over a stile onto an indistinct path which cuts across the field and emerges on the main A625 road. Cross the road with care and go left, passing a house on the right with a cart brake shoe hanging on the wall. Then, go right through a narrow gated stile alongside a stream and through fields to emerge on the lane adjacent to Hope station. On reaching the lane turn left and then right at the kissing gate, over the old goods yard to the station footbridge.

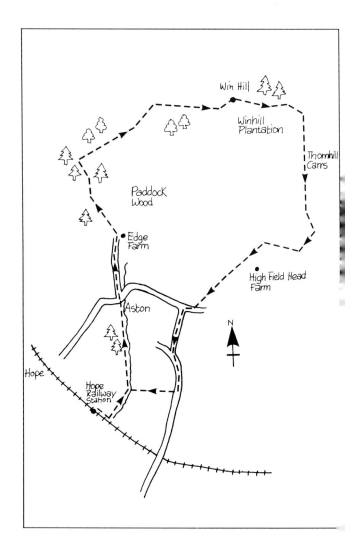

HOPE TO WIN HILL
CIRCULAR RAMBLE

Hope, a good half a mile from its station, is a delightful village which has a well dressing ceremony every year. This ancient Derbyshire custom probably dates back to Pagan times when spirits of the water were worshipped but it is now a Christian celebration. The wells in the village are dressed with pictures made of natural materials such as seeds and bark embedded on a clay background. It really is a work of art and involves dozens of villagers in intensive preparation in the hours leading up to the well dressing week. If you do not manage to visit Hope's well dressing week then there are several to choose from throughout the Peak District during the summer months.

Leave Hope station by the footpath which is reached from the Sheffield bound platform. The path runs alongside the line for a short distance to a kissing gate before turning left and entering fields. Follow the path alongside the willow bordered stream. The summit of Win Hill is clearly in view at this point. Pass through a number of fields, still alongside the stream, to a guide post by a bridge. Do not cross the bridge but follow the sign to Win Hill and continue ahead until you reach a lane at a junction by a barn.

Go left on the lane and then immediately right up another lane passing two green boxes. The lane begins to climb passing King's Haigh Farm. At Edge Farm, the lane bears left and becomes a muddy track signed to Hope Cross. Continue up the lane to a derelict barn.

Proceed ahead through a gate and skirt around a small plantation to emerge into a steeply sloping field. Here a tremendous view opens up along the Vale of Edale. In the right hand top corner of the field a ladder stile can be seen. However, your right of way is to the field boundary before you, then right, diagonally across the field up to the stile.

Impressive Views

Once over the stile there are a series of hollow ways leading up the hillside. Follow the right hand route, which is well worn and offering impressive views. Climb past a patch of gorse and wind battered hawthorns and the summit comes into view. Pass by a large cairn, then keep right at the second cairn, still heading directly for the top. At the third cairn turn right along the ridge path to the summit, marked by a Trig Point. The views are extensive. Continue ahead, in an easterly direction, and descend to twin ladder stiles. Cross over and continue downhill steeply into the wood.

Where a wall comes across the line of descent and the trees become coniferous, turn right and follow the wall. Beyond the woodland, there follows a magnificent high level stretch of cartway with lovely views over Bamford. At the concrete trough the cart track veers to the left. The hillside to your left begins to fall away steeply and Bamford village can be seen below. The cart road leads into a cutting and on emerging runs alongside a wall on your left to a gate. Here you will find a sign proclaiming that the way is private and that the footpath can be gained by following the wall to the right. Most ramblers follow this route to the large ladder stile just over a deep hollow way.

Cross the stile and go diagonally down the field towards a piece of fencing to the right of the gate in the wall. Reaching this point you will find a stile leading into a broad green lane with an embankment on the left hand side. Keep to this as the field narrows to a wet area by the next stile. Beyond this a narrow muddy lane leads soon to the road by Aston, emerging by two fine stone water troughs.

Go right at the road and continue to the next road junction and go left, either down the road or along the paralleling path. Go down the lane to Hallum Barn where a signpost points across the field to your right. Go over the stile and walk parallel to the power lines in a westward direction. The path is indistinct here but once over the brow a footbridge comes into view. Head for this and cross it to reach the signpost passed on the outward walk. Turn left and retrace your steps to Hope station.

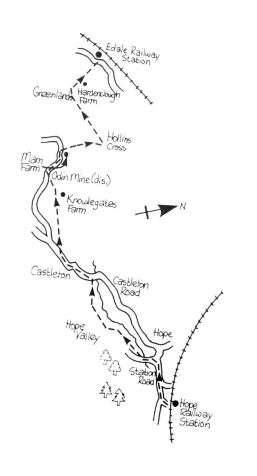

HOPE TO EDALE STATIONS VIA CASTLETON

This walk is in two parts, the first being a gentle ramble to Castleton where it is possible to catch a bus back to the turning for Hope railway station. The second section is more exacting, with a climb up to Hollins Cross and then down to Edale, a much longer stretch but with magnificent views. The choice is yours, the walk is very rewarding.

Follow the railway station access road down to the main A625 road where you turn right for a half mile or so of road walking to Hope village. There is a footway alongside the road. Just before Hope church bear left and follow this tarmac lane a short distance to Pindale Road then turn left. Go across the bridge, keeping right at the junction past the Pinfold and ascend to the seat for weary walkers. Go right here, through a stile, and follow the often muddy path right, along the Peakshole Water, partly fenced in at places. You will see the Blue Circle Cement complex to the left and soon you cross a stile and single track railway line to the works.

Just over the railway, the path rounds a little knoll of thorn trees and Peveril Castle and Mam Tor come into view. Head for the stile by the iron gate. Do not follow the line of the iron gates but keep with the stiles which soon bring the path close beside Peakhole Water. The squat tower of Castleton church comes into view. Continue on the path, which passes a reservoir on the right and soon enters a walled lane which is followed to its junction with the main road near Spital Bridge. Go left here into Castleton.

Castleton

Castleton has no shortage of places to take refreshment and

there are a number of gift shops. It has a rather fine old church, a daunting Peveril Castle and no fewer than four show caverns, Peak Cavern is the most accessible to this walk, being in the village itself. Until the prudish Victorians abridged the guide books, the yawning mouth of this cavern was referred to, even on maps, as the 'Devil's Arse'! For 'Blue John' devotees there are various collections on display in the village and the other caverns specialise in the mineral.

One local custom of interest is Oak Apple Day, 29 May, when a village King and Consort travel on horseback through the village to the market place where a garland is lifted from the King's shoulders and hoisted up to one of the pinnacles of the church tower. This festivity, which includes visits to local hostelries celebrates the restoration of the 'Good King Charles' centuries ago. Traditions die hard!

If returning to Hope the bus leaves from the small bus station. If continuing the walk to Edale, leave Castleton via the main road in the direction of Mam Tor. Opposite the Peak Cavern Car Park, go right along a signed footpath between two houses leading to open fields. Head for the white tree and so come alongside Odin Sitch. At the next stile there are some very fine examples of fossils in the wall, but please leave them for others to see. To the left is a view into the mouth of the Winnats Pass, a spectacular limestone gorge.

◀Although Castleton is frequently crowded with traffic and visitors the church in the centre of the village can be relied upon to provide a relative haven of peace and quiet. *Les Nixon*

Odin Mine

Continue by the wall until a stile is reached by a bridge and farm track. Go over the stile, but not over the bridge. Instead, continue forward with the stream on your right until a culvert is reached and the path crosses to the opposite side of the sitch, heading for Knowlegates Farm. Skirting the farm on the left, cross the farm access road and continue around the farm, bearing right up to a stile which takes you out of the farmland and onto the tumbled lower slopes of Mam Tor and the ravages of Odin Mine.

The path is obvious underfoot and after passing through an area of bracken, go over another stile to the old workings of the Odin Mine. The fenced enclosure to the right contains Knowles shaft, originally some 240 feet deep. The site of the horse worked winding engine can be determined by the shaft but even more fascinating, further along the path towards the old main road, is a crushing wheel, once used for crushing the minerals and rocks.

'The Shivering Mountain'

Follow the path to the remains of the main road, closed because of landslips and earth movements of Mam Tor, hence its name 'The Shivering Mountain'.

An information board explains about the slip and if you have time it is worth going to see the upper section of the devastated road. Walk up the road to the hairpin bend where your way is to the right along the track leading to Mam Farm. Go beyond the farm to a waymarked path on the left. The route skirts around the back of the cottages over a couple of stiles. Once over the latter keep left and

◀The amazing condition of the old A625 road which once snaked its way up the eastern slopes of Mam Tor. The road was closed to traffic in 1979. Directly above the runner can be clearly seen the footpath to Rushup Edge and Edale.

Les Nixon

begin the steady climb to Hollins Cross. The views down the valley are magnificent.

Hollins Cross

On reaching Hollins Cross take a breather at the viewfinder and ahead of you is Edale. Leave the ridge on the Edale side, slanting left towards the village in the distance. At the sign post and stile go left following the route marked Barber Booth, ignoring the route signed to Edale! Your route soon develops into a pleasant grassy hollow way. This becomes rougher with numerous hummocks, again the results of natural slippage. By a very prominent hillock the path crosses a stile and into a hollow way again. Beyond a further stile and gate the hollow way becomes a closely fenced path and bridleway which can get very muddy. This eventually goes down steeply to a gate at Greenlands Farm. At the gate go right into a lane which crosses a stream then swings right to meet another tarmac lane. Follow this down to the main road where you turn right, then first left for the railway station and village.

WALK FOURTEEN: Approximately 8/9 miles (13 km)

EDALE TO CHINLEY STATION

This is a classic walk by way of Jacob's Ladder and is by no means an easy task. The paths, however, are very clear and the views marvellous. Allow the best part of a day for this ramble.

Edale is the starting point of the Pennine Way and as such enjoys a tremendous popularity for such an isolated village. On some days you might find yourself getting off the train with one hundred others. Even so, the network of paths seem to absorb ramblers readily and once beyond the village it becomes very quiet for the most part.

The Peak Park Information Centre is open daily and is a matter of minutes from the station.

Leave the railway station platforms and bear left on the road for the top end of Edale, known as Grindsbrook Booth. Pass by the Rambler Inn, the Peak Park Information Centre and the church before reaching the Nag's Head public house, the shop, post office and small cafe. At this point you turn left along the Pennine Way Alternative Path which is waymarked and well trodden. Proceed at first by the stream onto open fields, then follow the waymarks to Broadlee Bank where the path splits, non too distinctly, but here is a sign. Go left and descend rapidly through fields to a track leading into Upper Booth. Go through the farmyard to the telephone kiosk and turn right along a track.

Jacob's Ladder

There is a mile or so of clear walking up the valley, passing Lee Farm, where there is an information display to your left. You can now begin to make out the great sweep of

69

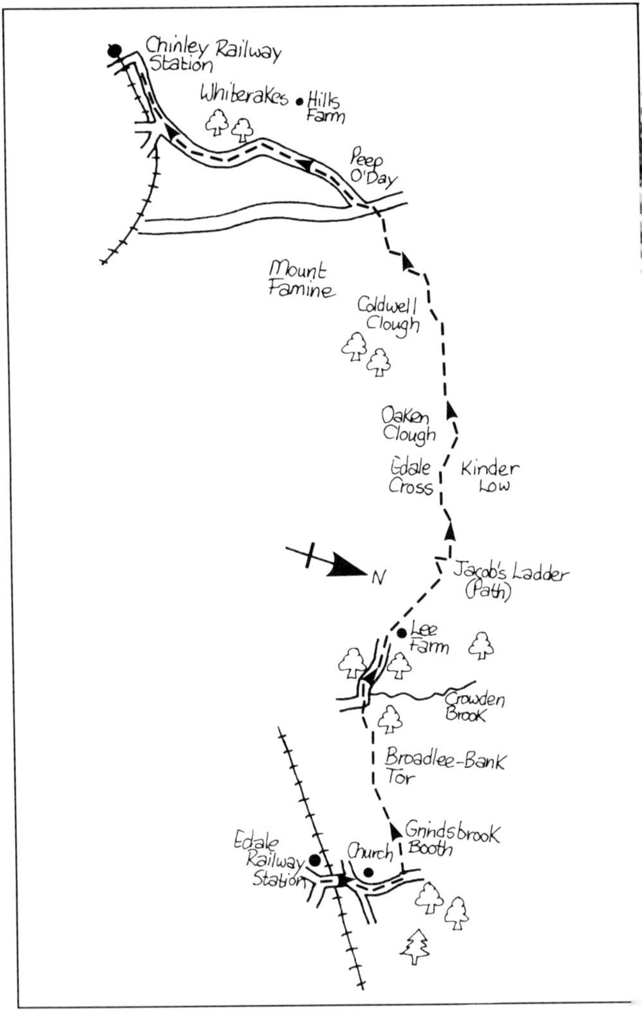

Chinley Railway Station

Whiberakes • Hills Farm

Peep O'Day

Mount Famine

Coldwell Clough

Oaken Clough

Edale Cross   Kinder Low

N

Jacob's Ladder (Path)

• Lee Farm

Crowden Brook

Broadlee-Bank Tor

Grindsbrook Booth

Edale Railway Station   • Church

the packhorse route zig zagging up the valley as it narrows. Cross the packhorse bridge and climb the pedestrian way up this steep hillside.

To your right are Edale Rocks and Kinder Low. Shortly, a well marked path leads off to the right. Do not turn right here, however, but continue ahead on the packhorse route beyond the gateway to its summit at Edale Cross, dated 1810 but thought to be much older. It is reckoned that the cross was a boundary marker for the Cistercian monks of Basingwerk Abbey.

At this point you have crossed the main watershed of England. Behind you all rivers flow to the Trent and North Sea. Ahead of you the rivers flow to the Mersey and Irish Sea. The valley to the south is the Sett and the prominent hills on the far side of the valley are South Head and Mount Famine with Chinley Churn beyond.

Follow this track down Oaken Clough, ignoring the path off to the right at Stoney Ford and continue for about a mile to Coldwell Clough Farm.

Mount Famine

Beyond the farm, as the lane bears right, go left instead down to a footbridge over the infant Sett and then steeply up beside a stream, which is crossed shortly, to join another path coming up from Hayfield. Go left at this junction and follow this route as it swings across the north flank of Mount Famine before joining the old Hayfield to Chapel road, now a green lane here. Mount Famine is an unusual name, the legend being that cattle brought to graze here never fattened.

Go over it and onto another path ahead, passing by an old quarry and onto the main A624 road. Go left here for a short distance then cross over into a quiet tarmac lane which you follow for well over a mile into Chinley where access to the station is on the right.

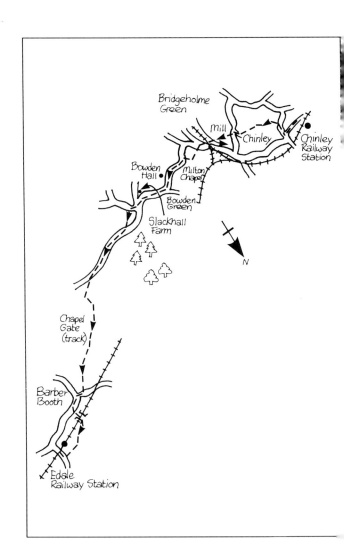

WALK FIFTEEN: Approximately 9 miles (15 km)

CHINLEY TO EDALE STATION

A day's ramble across fields and following old moorland tracks. The walk requires stamina as there are several climbs towards Rushup Edge.

It is possible to walk a much shorter distance to Chapel Milton returning via roads to Chinley.

On leaving Chinley railway station turn left and at the junction turn right down Station Road and then continue downwards along Green Lane to the bridge over Black Brook. Take the first turn left beyond it in the direction of the bleach works and at the car park go right at the entrance and a track leads off to the right of the more recent buildings to join the trackbed of the old Peak Forest Tramway. Go left here, passing by a number of buildings and as the track bears right before the sewerage works there is a path off to the left that follows the banks of the brook to a stile by Bridgeholme Mill.

Peak Forest Tramway

The Peak Forest Tramway was built in the early 1790s and ran until the year of the General Strike. Up to 60 wagons were hauled at any time by teams of horses. Built to link the quarries of Dove Holes and the canal basin at Buxworth this early industrial link carried limestone, coal and agricultural goods. The tramway was unusual in that it always used stone slab sleepers, some of which can be seen on the route.

Chapel Milton Viaduct

Cross the tarmac road and before you is a gap stile leading into the car park of the works.

Continue ahead between buildings to a gap stile by a gateway and then proceed towards the impressive double viaduct. Described as one of the greatest monuments to

73

Victorian Industrial England the viaduct is 780 feet long and 102 feet at its highest point. Opened by the Midland Railway as part of the Manchester and Derby railway in 1866 this line now carries quarry traffic only. The eastern viaduct was built as part of the Hope Valley line in the 1890s.

Cross the ladder stile and continue straight ahead. Under the viaduct cross over a green metal bridge. Note to the left a boundary marker for the Midland Railway.

You come out onto the main A625 road, with the Cross Keys public house to your left. Cross the road and go down the lane virtually opposite. On your left is an old farm cum post office. The post box is still to be seen in the farmhouse wall. There is no longer a post office here. As the lane curves left there is a stile on your left. If this is obstructed then the barred gate is the nearest diversion in to the field. Climb up the hill and the path leads to a stone stile beyond the hawthorn bush. Head slightly left here to the remains of a stile in a depleted hedge, ignoring the white stile slightly to your right. Continue to walk slightly left to the next field boundary, then bear left and follow the hedge to a stile by the hollybush and onwards to another stile leading into a wood.

Otters and Owls

Bear right here and the path soon leads to a tarmac lane where you turn left for a climb up to Bowden Head passing by Bowden Hall on your right. This leads up to a junction by a group of houses. Turn right and follow the lane to

The imposing viaducts of Chapel Milton. The one directly head of the photograher takes the railway line from Peak Forest to Chinley and Manchester whereas the one glimpsed the left swings round to make a connection with the Hope Valley line.   Les Nixon

Blackhall. On the left as you approach the main A625 road you will come across The Chestnut Centre, an Otter and Owl sanctuary. There is also a visitor centre and tea room, the latter being your last chance of refreshment for miles. Nearby is Ford Hall, once the home of William Bagshawe-the 'apostle of the Peak'. He spent much of his life promoting the non conformist church suffering persecution in the process.

On the hill ahead there is an ancient burial mound in a pasture known as 'Bendigo's Field'. It was here that one of the most famous of Victorian boxers, 'Bendigo', drew a crowd of 10,000 in 1837 to see him win a prize fight with Bill Looney, the latter name being quite appropriate for the sport in question.

Cross the main road and climb steeply up the tarmac lane. As it veers to the right continue ahead along a rough track which is clearly defined and eventually leads to the main road once again. At the road turn right and walk uphill to a short distance beyond the turning off to the right. Cross the road and go over the stile on the left leading to a well worn track. Follow this upwards with views to the left across the moorland and to the airshaft of the Cowburn Tunnel.

At the first main junction go left along an eroded moorland way. Soon, views of Edale valley appear and the path curves to the right and begins to descend more steeply. This section is known as Chapel Gate which literally means the way to Chapel, being Chapel-en-le-Frith.

◀The delightful hamlet at Ford Hall as seen from the grounds of the Chestnut Centre. In the winter the field in the foreground is frequently used as a nursery slope for skiers.

Les Nixon

At the bottom corner as the main track leads off to the right, you cross the stile on your left signed to Edale via Barber Booth. The path is well worn and crosses a stile ahead of you. There's a gap stile to your left. Go through and then head slightly right in the direction of the farm, continuing through three stiles.

Keep to the hedge on the left before the farm and cross over the stile to the left of the outbuildings and over another to find that you are now on the other side of the complex.

Barber Booth

Your way is slightly right to another stile, then cross the farm track and continue ahead along a very clear path to the tarmac lane. Turn right and walk the short distance to Barber Booth. At the bridge turn left to cross the infant river Noe and continue ahead passing the shop, rather than turning right. Turn left through a kissing gate along a well worn path signed to Grindsbrook Booth. Go over the railway bridge and turn right along the track. You will find a stile signed to Edale leading off the track. Follow this route along a green swathe of grass through two stiles. The path keeps to the hedge to the next stile and then bears slightly left across the field to another stile.

Go over the stile and continue ahead across the farm track. Your way is ahead to a gap stile. Go through it and proceed ahead, once again now keeping company with the hedge on your left. Cross another stile and then exit by way of a stile by the house on the left where you meet the tarmac road just before the Peak Park Information Centre. Go right here for the railway station.

The Peak National Park boundary stone adjacent to the Chestnut Centre owl and otter sanctuary.   *Les Nixon*

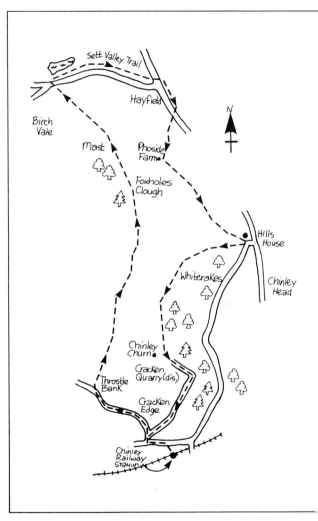

CHINLEY TO HAYFIELD CIRCULAR RAMBLE

Chinley station was once an important railway junction and in many respects lead to the growth of Chinley itself as a small town. The layout and size of the station itself was considerable and although rationalisation has taken place during recent years one can still imagine how busy it would have been at the beginning of the century.

On leaving the platform of Chinley station go left along the access path to the tarmac lane where you go left again. Follow this road upwards, gently at first, but then as it veers to the right becoming steeper. Pass by Dryclough Farm and further up, Throstles Farm. After this point you will see, as the road begins to level out, a rough track leading off to the right. Go right here up the track, through a barred gate, then keeping to the drystone wall on the left, climb up to a double gate with adjacent stiles. The views over the Goyt Valley and to New Mills are exceptionally good here.

The track becomes much wider for a time, passing through another gate, and continuing ahead. The views into the Sett Valley now become clearer. You come to a meeting of bridleways. Go ahead and to the left, keeping the drystone wall to your left. The track descends with equally impressive views and begins to move gently away from the wall across the moorland, with the television transmission mast slightly to your left in the foreground. You meet another drystone wall, now on your right. Continue to descend passing through a gate and meeting a track. Continue downhill along the track to meet the main A6015 road at the Grouse Inn, Birch Vale.

Sett Valley Trail

Cross the road and opposite is a path leading to the Sett Valley Trail. Turn right and follow the trail former the short distance to Hayfield. This railway once carried thousands of passengers to Hayfield for pleasure, now they walk. It also served the cotton mills of the valley which at one time would have been a significant feature.

Pass by the cycle hire and information centre situated at the old station. Buses leave here for Glossop, New Mill and Stockport if you decide to finish the walk at this stage.

Hayfield

Cross the main road into the older part of the village passing by the church, cafes and inns. Hayfield is the home of the Kinder Trespass celebrations and a Jazz Festival. In September each year there are also local sheep dog trial at nearby Little Hayfield. Turn right and walk up Church Street, but as the road bears right to re join the main by pass road, continue ahead along the old road. This passe a number of houses and as it begins to climb steeply, go right along a track marked to Smithfold Farm. This leac to the main A624 road, which you cross, continuing along the track signed to Phoside Farm.

As you approach the farm you go right in front of the barn, go over a stile, then sharp left and left again at the rear of the building passing between it and the remains of an old mill. Cross the stream and the path leads up through the wood to a stiles. Cross it and continue ahead with the drystone wall on your left. Go through a gate into the next field and continue ahead once again.

Peep-O-Day

The path becomes less distinct by Far Phoside but becomes clearer as you follow the sunken path leading upwards from the truncated telegraph pole. Go through the fenced section spanning the bog and then through a gateway onto drier land. Your path is ahead, across the brook and then curving away to a stile and gate. Continue ahead with the drystone wall to your left to another coralled section in an even boggier area and then through the gap in the wall. The path leads slightly left here, but it is none too clear. Aim for the telegraph poles and then you will see a drystone wall and open gateway by Peep-O-Day Farm, named no doubt because of the limited daylight inside.

Turn right here up the rough track and at the first fork take to lower, left hand way. The track then dips done before a final climb towards Hills Farm. Go left in the dip, through the gate and begin to climb once again, to pass by Whiterakes on your left. The path now winds up to a stile leading into the remains of a disused quarry. Cross another stile to an extension of the quarry and from here onwards more care is required because the path narrows as it descends beneath a scree slope.

You can see your way ahead along an old track following the field boundary. At the junction before you, go left down the sunken track and then keep to it to the field corner. The track now turns right, descending towards Cracken Edge Farm. Just beyond the turn for the farm there's a stile on the left. Go over it and follow the steep and winding path down to another stile. Continue downhill to another stile between two gardens and this path leads you to a tarmac road. Turn right for the station.

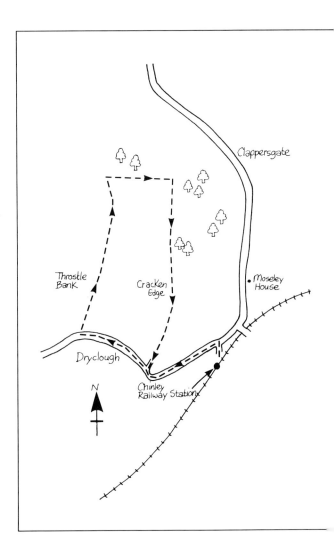

Clappersgate

Throstle
Bank

Cracken
Edge

Moseley
House

Dryclough

N

Chinley
Railway Station

CHINLEY TO CRACKEN EDGE CIRCULAR RAMBLE

A short walk offering good views across Chinley. One or two steep climbs but otherwise an easy walk taking about one hour.

Walk up the steps from Chinley station platform and turn left. At the tarmac lane turn left again and follow this up as in Walk Sixteen by Dryclough Farm.

Shortly afterwards there is a stile on the left. Climb up the road bank and cross it. Follow the sunken path up the old 'road' up to the disused Cracken Quarry.

Quarrying

This quarry, like others in the area, produced high quality paving flags and roofing slates. Some of the quarry faces and the remaining spoil can be observed although nature is taking over once again. The path itself uses one of the early tramroads for removing rock to wagons. Above the quarry is the point known as Chinley Churn, possibly being the burial place of an ancient British chieftain.

Keep to this path until it reaches a stile. Cross this and take a breather while you look across to the Goyt and Whaley Bridge. Walk a short distance through rough ground then as the path curves left go right down a wet section of track to join the main track along the field boundary. This turns right and begins to descend gradually. Follow this down to the tarmac lane once again. Turn left and just beyond where the road turns left there is an opening into a small park with seats overlooking Chinley. The path leads slightly right through the park and down to a white gate. Go through it and cross the footbridge across the railway. Go left at the other side to the entrance to the station.

86

CHINLEY TO WHALEY BRIDGE CIRCULAR RAMBLE

A walk through early industrialisation, from Buxworth to Whaley Bridge by way of the Peak Forest canals, returning mainly through fields. Easy walking with very few climbs.

From the platform of Chinley station walk up the steps and turn right. At the road turn right and walk along this street until you reach the footbridge where you turn right again. Cross the bridge and go through the gate. Go through the recreational area, the path now leading up to a gateway and tarmac road. Go left here and at the junction continue ahead rather than turning right.

This soon becomes a track. Continue ahead and after passing a group of houses the track forks. Go left and there are three gates before you and Cotebank Farm to your right up the hill. Go through the one directly ahead, with a gap stile adjacent to it. The main track now leads to a farm, but just before the hawthorn bush you turn left, down a wet area of ground to a walled track leading downhill to Buxworth. At the end of the walled section go over a stile and walk across rough ground to the road seen between the houses below.

The walk from Chinley seen top right, involves a fairly lengthy climb along a minor Tarmac road to Dry Clough Farm, seen in the middle of the picture. At this point walkers take the stile and turn right to follow the footpath on to Cracken Edge.
                                                                    Les Nixon

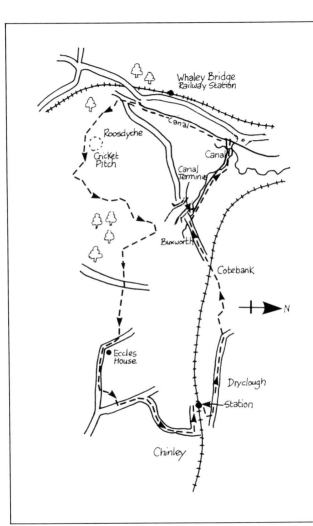

Buxworth

At the main B6062 road turn right and this leads you under the railway to the school where you turn left down to The Navigation public house. Turn right here to Buxworth Wharf which is being restored. The village name has always been a source of contention. It probably derives from a Ralph Bugge, a bailiff of the Peak Forest in the mid 13th century. Little did he know that it would lead to ridicule and eventually to the changing of 'gs' to 'x'. Led by the local clergyman in the late 1920s, the parishioners petitioned Parliament for a change of name and much to everyone's surprise, permission was granted. It became such a good story that the Punch magazine devoted much attention to the issue.

The canal terminus is fascinating. This would have been a busy inland port accommodating up to 20 narrow boats at any one time. The tramways, wharfs and docks are presently being restored and what a pleasant sight it will be when boats return.

Whaley Bridge

The way is straightforward now. Follow the canal towpath to its junction with the Peak Forest Canal. Cross over the Buxworth Branch by way of the footbridge and then continue along the Peak Forest towpath to the transhipment shed at Whaley Bridge. It was here that goods from the Peak Forest Canal were transferred to wagons for distribution. From the early 1830s onwards the Cromford and High Peak Railway carried traffic across the Peak District to Cromford. The remains of the railway, which operated

through Whaley Bridge until the late 1950s, can be seen in several places. The trucks were drawn at first by horse but then steam power was introduced within the first decade. What a marvellous feat of engineering.

From the transhipment shed go straight across the road and continue ahead passing by the car park on the left. Go over the recently restored bridge with old rails and then walk up one of the original inclines. When you reach the road go left and left again. Within a matter of steps there is a walled tarmac path up to the right.

Go up this and at the next road go left. Go left again and as this curves to the right it soon becomes a rougher track.

The Roosdyche

You pass by the Roosdyche, something of a local mystery. Some say that it was once the scene of chariot races during Roman times, others point to it being a natural phenomenon, possibly carved out during a previous Ice Age. Keep ahead and the track passes the cricket ground on your left and then in the corner of the field you come to a stile next to a barred gate. Cross this and keep to the walled garden on your right by the secluded Horwich House. At the corner of this field there is a stile leading onto the road.

Go left here and follow this track upwards until it bears sharp left. Ahead of you is Buxworth. Go right at this point, crossing into a field and then descending gently to the workings of an old quarry. Go beyond the quarry to a barred gate before a number of cottages. Do not go through the gate but instead turn right through a gateway. You are

◀Where railway and canal once met at Whaley Bridge. The present day scene shows numerous pleasure craft in the canal basin but in olden days it was the trans-shipment point between the canal and the Cromford and High Peak Railway.

Les Nixon

now moving away from the village. Walk diagonally across the field to the top left hand corner. The path is not clear here and leads into wetter ground the closer you come to the field boundary. There is, however, a stone stile leading into the next field. Go over it and cut right across to the field boundary on the right. Follow this field boundary uphill towards the top of the field but bear left near the top to meet a stile in a somewhat precarious condition, which leads onto a track.

Cross this and you will see there are two tracks ahead. Take the left hand path where you will find a stile next to a barred gate. Cross it and walk along this delightful green lane, through two gateways in succession to a group of houses, known as Eccles Fold, and a tarmac lane. Go right here and pass by Eccles House on the left. On reaching an arbour of trees on the left cross the stone stile on the left and this leads down to another stile by a house. Cross it and follow the lane around to the right. At the junction go left into Chinley. Take care in places as there is no footpath. Fortunately, as you pass through Whitehough you pass by the Oddfellows Arms and Old Hall Inn. This road leads up to Chinley and the railway station.

THE HOPE VALLEY LINE

The Hope Valley line, or the Dore and Chinley line as its promoters called it, came late to the railway map of Derbyshire and came perilously close to leaving early. Running as it does, east–west, it offers an easy passage through the southern edge of the Pennines apart from the towering bulk of Cowburn in the west and the gritstone edges in the east.

The railway pioneers of the late 1820s sought to overcome these obstacles by the means of steep inclined planes, stationary engines and miles of rope. Indeed, the earliest railway scheme for a line from Sheffield to Manchester should have come this way, winding its trains out of the Sheaf Valley to Strawberry Lea, then down the other side to Grindleford for an easy run to Upper Booth in Edale. After a climb to Cowburn and a precipitous descent to Chapel Milton the line would then join the Peak Forest Tramway, suitably converted to a railway via Stockport to Manchester.

Great Setback

This was a prophetic scheme in many ways but at the time George Stephenson, the engineer for the company, was so busily engaged with other projects that he could not devote the time to this one and the survey and design was poor. Matters were already at a low ebb with the Parliamentary Committee considering the scheme when a diligent participant, noting that passengers were to be wound down the incline to Chapel Milton in a tunnel, asked what would happen if the rope broke. The response that there would be burly men on hand to sprag the wheels was not only a serious indictment of railway safety methods of the day but also damned the Sheffield and Manchester route via the above mentioned route. The villages of the Hope Valley were to wait a further 60 years before they saw their railway come to fruition.

Decades of Schemes

There were, however, numerous schemes proposed ranging from madcap schemes such as London North Western company's proposal across the face of Mam Tor to what would have been England's longest narrow gauge line, the Sheffield and Buxton. The Manchester, Buxton, Matlock and Midlands Junction sought to come via Hope having been thwarted at Haddon Hall. The Cavendish influence in Buxton was stronger, however, and the line went by Bakewell. Later, the Midland Railway proposed several links between Bakewell and Sheffield by way of Grindleford with branches to Castleton but none came to fruition.

In the 1880s England entered the final railway building mania. Out of this conflagration came the Great Central Railway's line from Sheffield to London and from it also came the Midland Railway Company's riposte, a line from Sheffield to Manchester as a direct competitor to the Great Central route via Penistone.

Tunnels

In fact, by the mid 1880s the Midland had only to build relatively short link between Dore and Chinley to secure its objective, but that link involved two enormous tunnels Cowburn at the western end and Totley in the east. Altogether, over a quarter of the new line was in tunnel. Cowburn at 2 miles and 182 yards was Britain's ninth longest and Totley at 3 miles and 950 yards the second longest, beaten only by the Severn Tunnel if the Circle Line is discounted! Construction began in 1888 and the line finally opened in 1894.

For some reason, having built the line, the Midland never seriously exploited the competitive edge it had gained. Even in 1910, possible the heyday of the company, there were only five express trains in each direction, compared with the Great Central's twelve.

Thus the line settled into a fairly mundane existence as the secondary route between Sheffield and Manchester. The obvious link between Bakewell and the new line at Grindleford was proposed but never built and in the 1920s the railway company ran buses on the route instead. Similarly, rail links to Castleton from Hope were proposed but never built. Two branches were progressed. One opened in 1927 to serve the Blue Circle Cement Works near Hope and this survives. The other enjoyed two existences, first from 1903 to 1914 when it ran from Bamford to Birchinlee to serve the building of the Howden and Derwent reservoirs, then secondly from 1935 to 1945 for the building of Ladybower reservoir.

With nationalisation and the later Beeching Plan for "rationalisation" the line was marked down for closure to passenger traffic. Amazingly, the closure of most of the stations was approved but with the proviso that Edale and Hope be kept open, the former because of the consequence of visitor impact with particular reference to ramblers. Not surprisingly this compromise did not endear itself to British Rail and the end result was the retention of the entire line with a closure of the Woodhead route instead.

The Hope Valley line is now entering a resurgence, with improved local services, and new through express services between East Anglia & Liverpool and Nottingham & Blackpool using new rolling stock. This has been made possible with the construction of two new lines, the Hazel Grove Chord which connects the Midland Route to Manchester with the ex LNWR Buxton–Manchester route and the Windsor Link in Manchester which enables trains from Manchester Piccadilly to access the route from Manchester

Victoria to Blackpool. After 154 years Stephenson's Sheffield and Manchester railway via the Hope Valley and Stockport is a reality.

Printed by Bayliss Printing Company, Stanley Street, Worksop Notts. S81 7HX